lasticine
balloon
everal small tins
ome heavy tinfoil
bicycle pump and adapter
playball or football bladder
arden canes
rinking straws
n egg, hard-boiled
large handkerchief
wo table-tennis balls
ome strong paper
wo iron nails
ome pins

2020
£1.50

G000270912

Series 621

*What **is** Air? Can it be weighed? Why does the wind blow? How does an aeroplane rise into the air? Why does an astronaut wear a special suit?*

In this fascinating book you will find the answers to these and many other questions about Air, the way it behaves, and how essential it is to Life. And you will learn, too, how the scientist finds these answers— by experiment.

All the materials needed are simple and safe, and can be easily obtained.

The Publishers wish to acknowledge the helpful interest and encouragement given by J. Cottam, Dip.Ed. (Headmaster) in the early stages of planning this series.

A Ladybird Junior Science Book

AIR, WIND and FLIGHT

by F. E. NEWING, B.Sc. *and* RICHARD BOWOOD
with illustrations by J. H. WINGFIELD

Ladybird Books Ltd Loughborough

We must have Air

Why does a man wear a special space-suit when he goes beyond the earth's atmosphere? Why does a deep-sea diver wear a similar kind of suit? How do aeroplanes fly? Why does the wind blow?

All these questions are concerned with air, which we cannot see, taste or smell, but without which we cannot live. The scientists who design the space-suit, the aeroplane or the diver's suit, solve problems about air by experiment. In this book you will be able to find out something about air and the way it behaves, and, like the scientist, you can do it by experiment.

Just as a fish cannot live out of water, so we cannot live without air. The space-man and the diver must take their air with them. Waking and sleeping, we breathe air. Sometimes we breathe lightly, sometimes deeply. You can measure how much air you breathe.

You need a bucket or bowl full of water, several pint milk bottles, and a length of rubber tubing. Fill the bottles under water and turn them upside-down. Place the rubber tube under one of the bottles, take a

deep breath and blow through the tube into it. The air will force the water from the bottle. When you have filled the bottle with air, hold your breath and put the tube into another bottle and blow again. In this way you can find how many pints of air you have breathed out.

4

0 7214 0120 1

Air is Real

For this experiment you need a small funnel, a bottle, and some plasticine. Fill the bottle about two-thirds full of water and seal the funnel into the neck with plasticine. Pour some water into the funnel. The water will either not run into the bottle at all, or only in small spurts. Now make a hole through the plasticine with a pin and see what happens.

For the next experiment fill a bowl with water and put a tumbler completely under the water so that it fills. Hold this upside down with one hand and with the other push another tumbler, open end downwards, into the water. Put the second tumbler under the first and tilt it so that the air bubbles up into the first one. You will see that the water in the first tumbler is driven out by the air rising from the second. At the same time, the second tumbler fills with water.

These experiments show that air is *real*, and takes up space. The water can only go into the bottle through the funnel if the air can go somewhere else—up through

Air goes in

Milk comes out

the pinhole. In the second experiment the water must make room for the air. This is why, when you pour liquid from a sealed tin you must make *two* holes, one for the liquid to come out and the other for the air to go in to take its place.

"Light as Air"

We have found that air is a real thing. This being so, it should weigh something. Does air weigh anything? To find out you must make some scales, or a *balance*. Scientists use a special delicate instrument, but you can make a simple balance which will weigh air quite well.

Get a light strip of wood, about 910 mm to 1.2 m long, and find its centre by balancing it across your finger. Make a hole at this point and hang the strip by a piece of thread through the hole. You have made a *balance beam*. Make a hole near each end. Hang a tin can at one end with three strings. Let the air out of a football bladder, or a playball if it is the kind you can let down, and fix an adapter in the end of the tube, as in the picture. (You can get one at a sports shop.) Hang the bladder on the other end of the balance.

Pour sand, rice, or something like that, into the can to balance the weight of the bladder. Now take the bladder off, blow it up hard and hang it on the balance again, with the adapter still in. You will find that you will have to put more weight into the tin to restore the balance of the beam. The weight of the sand or rice you have to put in, represents the weight of air put into the bladder.

So air does weigh something, if not very much. In fact, the weight of air in an ordinary room is about the same as a bag of coal—a hundredweight (51 kg).

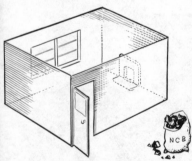

A Roomful of Air weighs about the same as a Bag of Coal

8

The Air we Breathe

When we breathe, air is drawn into our nose or mouth, goes down our windpipe and enters our lungs. These are not hollow like football bladders, but are more like two sponges. In the lungs, part of the air we have breathed does something necessary to our blood.

Air is a mixture of *gases*, the name given to everything which is neither a solid nor a liquid. In the lungs we use some of the *oxygen*, one of the gases in the air. Oxygen forms about one-fifth of the air, and most of the remaining four-fifths is a gas called *nitrogen*. Air also contains very, very small quantities of several other gases.

When we breathe out we expel any unused oxygen, together with the nitrogen, which we do not use. But there is also another gas, called *carbon dioxide*, which has been made in the body.

You can show that carbon dioxide is formed in your body by blowing out through a straw into *lime water*, which you can buy at the chemist for a few pence. It is quite harmless. When carbon dioxide is passed through it, the lime water turns cloudy or milky.

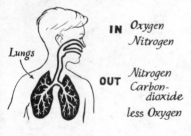

IN Oxygen
Nitrogen

OUT Nitrogen
Carbon-
dioxide
less Oxygen

Lungs

This is the experiment the children in the picture are doing, to show that when oxygen is used by the body carbon dioxide is produced. You will have to blow quite a lot to make the lime water turn milky, because we do not produce much carbon dioxide in each breath.

10

Air and Burning

For this experiment you need a piece of candle, a soup-plate, and several wide-necked jars of different sizes. Stick the candle to the plate with plasticine and light it. Pour water into the plate and put a small jar over it and start counting in seconds.

Make a note of the number of seconds you have counted when the candle goes out. Repeat the experiment with the larger jars and record the number of seconds the candle burns in each case. Make sure your candle-flame does not touch the glass.

If you watch carefully you will notice three things. The candle goes out; it burns longer in the larger jars; and water goes up into the jars as the candle burns.

The candle went out when it had used all the oxygen in the air in the jar, because without oxygen it could not burn. It burned longer in the larger jars because there was more air, and so more oxygen. Anything which burns must have oxygen. That is why a camp fire will burn better when plenty of air can flow through it.

Why did the water go up into the jar as the candle burned? One of the reasons was that the oxygen used formed carbon dioxide, which dissolves in water. As it dissolved there was space left in the jar, which the water had to occupy.

12

Air in Water

Your body uses oxygen and makes carbon dioxide, just as a candle uses oxygen when it burns. All living things use oxygen, to *burn* the food they eat to maintain life, though it is quite a different kind of burning from a candle flame. A fish uses oxygen in the same way, even though it lives under water. It takes the oxygen which is dissolved in the water through its gills.

You can show that there is oxygen in water by the following experiment. When iron rusts it joins with oxygen and forms a red powder, and without oxygen iron will not rust. Get two bright, *clean* iron nails and two medicine bottles. Drop a nail into each, and fill one completely with cold water from the tap. Then ask someone to fill the other with water which has recently boiled *and been allowed to cool*. Cork both bottles tightly and label them, 'Boiled' and 'Unboiled'.

Leave the bottles for several days and then examine them. One nail will show traces of rust, the other will not. Which nail rusted, and why?

The nail which did *not* rust will be in the boiled water, because the boiling drove out the oxygen. There was no oxygen in the water to rust the nail.

Fill a tumbler with water and leave it overnight in a warm room. In the morning you will find tiny bubbles of air on the inside of the glass. This is air set free from the water by the warmth of the room.

14

Squeezing Air

Fill a medicine bottle right to the top with cold water, make a plasticine cork round a drinking straw and fix it in the neck so that the bottle is sealed. Try to blow down the straw. If the bottle is completely full and properly sealed it is impossible.

Now take off the plasticine, pour away about half of the water and replace the plasticine and straw, with the end of the straw under the water. Now blow into the bottle for as long as you can—and see what happens when you take your mouth away.

Why, when the bottle was *full* of water, was it impossible to blow into it? Why, when it was *half full* of air, could you get some more air in? The reason is that when you blew into the bottle containing air you squeezed up, or *compressed*, the air, by forcing more air into the same space. But water cannot be compressed, so when you tried to blow into the bottle full of water there was no room for the air.

This shows an important scientific fact—gases can be

compressed, or squeezed into a smaller space. When you blew into the *half full* bottle you compressed the air inside. When you took your mouth away the air stretched or *expanded* again to its normal size and forced some of the water up the straw. Air, and all other gases, can be compressed into cylinders to be used when needed.

Air Pressure

Put an empty balloon inside a plastic beaker, and, keeping it inside, blow it up and squeeze the neck so that the air cannot come out. Lift the balloon, and the beaker will come with it. Let the air out very gradually and see when the beaker falls off.

Why did the beaker lift up with the balloon?

Put your fingers inside the empty beaker, pressing outwards, and lift it up. You have to *press outwards* to lift the beaker. That is exactly what the air in the balloon was doing: it was pressing outwards against the sides of the beaker.

You compressed air inside the balloon, and the more you compressed it the more it pressed outwards. When you pump up a bicycle tyre you test the outward push of the air in the tyre with your thumb, and the more air you pump in the more strongly the air pushes outwards and the 'harder' the tyre becomes.

The air all around us is always pressing in every direction. When you think about it, it is very lucky for us that air does press all around us. If two children push with equal force on opposite sides of a friend, he will stay still. If one stops pushing, he will tumble down. If air only pushed one way we would tumble down.

18

The Egg and the Bottle

Boil a small egg for ten minutes (until it is hard-boiled). Cool it under the cold tap and take the shell off carefully. Find a bottle with the neck slightly smaller than the egg; a quart milk bottle is ideal. Sit the egg on the bottle, pointed end down. Think about it for a moment. The egg is being held by the bottle, and the air inside the bottle and the air outside are pressing equally on the egg.

Lift up the egg and drop two lighted matches into the bottle. Put the egg back and watch. The matches will go out quickly, because they use up the oxygen in the bottle.

Gradually the egg will squeeze through the neck of the bottle. Why? The burning matches use some of the air, and decrease the air pressure inside, so the air pressure outside is greater and *pushes* the egg through the neck. This shows that air *presses*, and quite strongly, too.

You can use air pressure to get the egg out of the bottle, providing it is not too tight a fit. This time

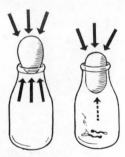

you must make the pressure inside greater than it is outside. Hold the bottle up and blow into it as hard as you can past the egg. This will build up the pressure inside and make it strong enough to force the egg out again.

More Experiments on Air Pressure

Fill a tumbler right to the top with water and carefully slide any piece of smooth cardboard, such as a post card, over the top so that there is no air under the card. Hold your hand on the card and turn the tumbler upside down. Take your hand away and the card should stay in position. Why? Because the pressure of the air upwards, against the card, is greater than the pressure of the water downwards. (It is wise to do this over the sink.)

If you can find two pieces of smooth plastic, put a little water on one and press the other firmly against it. Try to separate them. Do you see why they 'stick' together? It is the pressure of the air again. There is no air between them to press outwards, and you will have to slide them apart. Rubber suckers for hanging hooks or ash-trays in motor cars stick firmly for the same reason.

When fruit is bottled it is heated in the bottle and the lid is put on while it is hot. The heating expands the air so that most of it is driven out of the bottle. When it

cools there is little air in the bottle to press outwards, so the lid is kept tightly in position by the pressure of the air outside. A new pot of jam from the shop often has to be pierced with a pin before you can open it—to let air in so that the pressure on both sides of the lid is the same.

22

The Syphon

The picture shows how you can clean an aquarium by syphoning out some of the water with a rubber tube. Hold the tube under the water until all the air has bubbled out. Then pinch one end tightly and bring it over the side until the end is below the water in the tank. Then let the end go and the water will flow out.

This is a good way to take water from an aquarium; it does not disturb the fish and you can use the end as a vacuum cleaner. If you have tadpoles or any very small fish, watch that they are not syphoned through the tube, unless you want to remove them painlessly into another jar.

You can find out more about the action of a syphon by using two jars and a rubber tube. Fill one jar with water, and fill the tube as well, as described above. Syphon some water into the lower jar, and, keeping the ends of the tube under the water in each jar, raise and lower one of them. See when the water flows fastest, when it flows backwards, and when it stops flowing. What happens when you let some air into the tube?

The syphon is a useful method of emptying anything which has not got a tap, such as a heavy water barrel. Some washing machines are also emptied by this method.

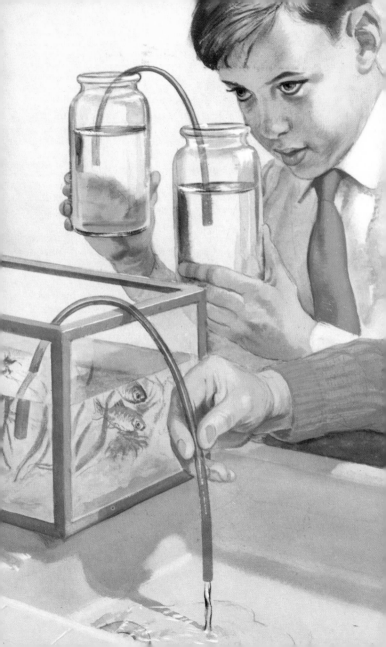

The Wind

If you unscrew the valve of a bicycle tyre the air rushes out. The same happens when you release a blown-up balloon. In both cases air moves from the place where the pressure is *high* to the place where it is *low*.

The air around us presses in all directions all the time, but the pressure is not always the same. Air will flow from a place where the pressure is high to one where it is lower, just as it flows from the bicycle tyre or balloon.

Wind is air on the move, and the greater the difference between the high pressure and the low, the faster it moves, or the harder the wind blows.

You can tell from which direction the wind blows by making a weather vane. Close one end of a short piece of drinking straw with a dab of sealing wax. Stick another piece of straw across the upright with an arrow on one end and a 'tail' on the other. This is a weather vane.

Put a cork on a knitting needle and stick four match sticks on to it, with the points of the compass cut out of thin card slipped into slits, or glued, to the ends of the matches. Now stick the end of the needle into a cork or board and balance the weather vane on the other end.

Take the weather vane outside, find out the North and hold it with your 'north' pointing that way. The arrow will be turned by the wind and will show you from which direction it is blowing.

26

The Barometer

The pressure of the air is measured by a *barometer;* as the pressure changes the needle moves round the dial. Since air pressure is one of the things which affect the weather, a barometer is a useful guide to weather changes.

You can make a simple kind of barometer with a bottle and a dish or tin lid. Put two pieces of wood in the dish to raise the rim of the bottle clear of the bottom of the dish. Fill the bottle with water, hold the dish over the top and turn the bottle upside-down carefully, but quickly. Some of the water will come out, so watch where you do it.

Put the bottle on a shelf where it can be left, such as in a shed or outhouse. Tilt the bottle slightly to let some more air in, until it is about a third full of air. Stick a piece of gummed paper on the bottle and mark the level of the water.

You have made a barometer which will show changes in the pressure of the air. When the pressure increases on the water in the dish, it forces the water in the bottle up, or, as we say, the *barometer rises*. When the pressure lessens on the water in the dish, the water in the bottle falls—the *barometer falls*.

With all barometers it usually means better weather when it rises and worse when it falls.

Your barometer must be set up in a cool place, because changes in temperature will affect it as well as changes in the pressure of the air.

Hot and Cold Air

When air is warmed it expands, becomes less dense, and takes up more space. A cork is less dense than water so it floats. A coin is more dense, so it sinks.

The picture shows the air in the tin on the right being warmed by the candle flame. The expanding air escapes as shown by the arrows and that which remains becomes less dense than the air in the other tin. The right hand tin therefore rises.

You can do the experiment shown by setting up the balance you used in the experiment on page 8 and hanging an empty tin—the larger the better—*upside down* on each end. Balance them exactly by sliding a small piece of wire along the balance arm. Put a short piece of candle below one of the tins and light it. Watch carefully. The tin over the candle goes up, making the balance tip. This experiment proves that warm air is less dense than cold air.

The first balloons were filled with hot air to make them rise. A small fire heated the air, which rose, filled the balloon, and up it went.

For another experiment, to show that hot air rises, you can make a hot-air fan from a circle of firm metal foil, cut and bent as you see in the picture. Balanced on a piece of bent wire, it is made to spin round by the warm air rising from the candle.

Insulation

For this experiment you need two tins with lids, a box or carton, and some packing—old rags, shredded newspaper, or sawdust. Put one tin in the box packed round loosely with rags, paper or sawdust, and stand the other tin in the open. Fill them both with hot water and put on the lids. Cover the tin in the box with more packing.

Wait until the water in the exposed tin is cool and then uncover the other. Why is the water in that tin still quite warm?

Think about the exposed tin first. The hot water warmed the air around it, so it became lighter and drifted, or was blown away, to be replaced by cold air. This in turn was warmed, drifted up and so continued to take the heat away from the tin.

The other tin also warmed the air around itself, but this air could not get away; it was trapped round the tin by the packing, and so the water remained hot much longer than in the other tin.

The packing round the tin in the box is called *insulation*. By trapping a layer of air around anything,  or by *insulating* it, you keep it warm. The hot water tank in your house may have an insulating jacket, to save wasting heat. Animals have fur, birds have feathers, you wear clothes—all for the same purpose, to keep a layer of air trapped next to the skin for warmth.

32

Moving Air

This experiment will give you something to puzzle about, and it shows a very interesting and a very important fact about the behaviour of air.

Make two paper flags on long pins and set them up in a piece of wood about 50 mm apart. Curve the flags inwards, as the boy has done in the picture.

Direct a straw between the flags and try to blow them apart. You cannot! Blow harder and what do you notice? The harder you blow the more firmly the flags come *together*. You would think they would go further apart.

Why is this? Think it out as a scientist would, reasoning step by step. Things only move if they are pushed or pulled. They move in the direction they are being pushed or pulled. Your two flags moved *closer together*. So they were pushed together—by your blowing between them. Why did they not blow *apart*?

The reason is that the moving stream of air made by your blowing produced a *lower pressure* between the flags.

The *greater pressure* of the air outside them pushed them together. In the picture the girl is doing a similar experiment with ping-pong balls.

The movement of air over the specially-shaped wings of a bird or aeroplane is essential to their flight.

34

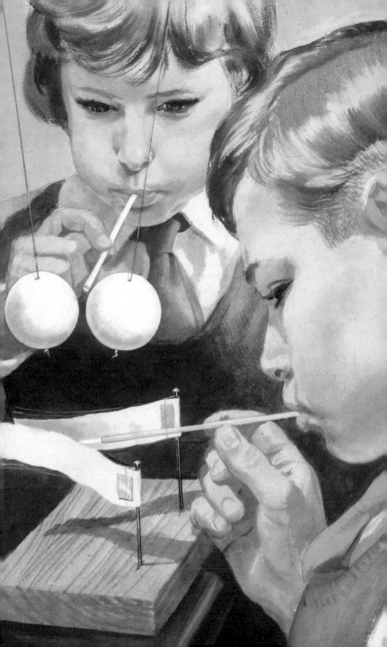

Air and 'Lift'

In the last experiments you showed that a stream of moving air produces low pressure. Here are two more experiments, which will help you to understand something about flight.

Push a pin through a piece of card, point upwards, and put a cotton reel over the top so that the pin is in the centre of the hole. Hold the card in position with your finger, blow downwards through the hole in the cotton reel, preferably with your lips close to the hole, and take your finger away. The card stays. Do it again, trying to blow the card away—it still stays.

Do you know the reason? It is because the moving air above the card produces a lower pressure than that of the air below. This holds the card firmly in place.

Tuck a strip of paper into a book and blow over the top of it. You would think the paper would be blown downwards, but now you will expect the opposite to happen. Because you blow *along* the top of the paper there is lower pressure above the strip of paper, and higher pressure beneath it, so up it goes.

This is what the airman calls *lift*. It means that

something heavier than air—paper, a bird, a glider—is lifted up when air moves past it. You have seen birds staying quite still high in the air, wings outstretched. They are using this *lift*, caused by different air pressures, against their wings. The man flying a glider is using that same *lift* to keep him in the air.

36

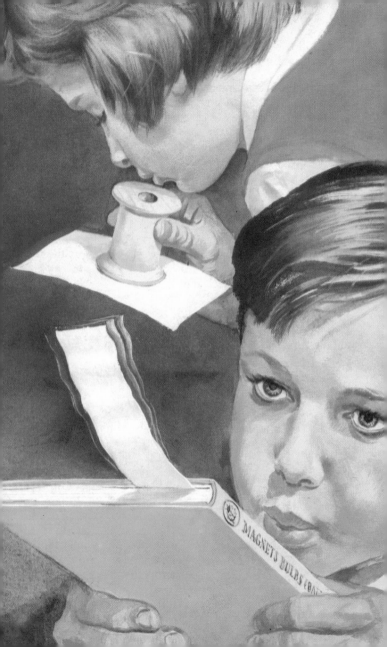

The Shape of Wings

In your experiments you have obtained *lift* by blowing, and the stream of moving air has always been on one side of the paper or card only. But with the wing of a bird, a glider, or an aeroplane the moving air is on *both* sides; so how does this produce *lift*? Has the shape of the wing anything to do with it?

You can find this out by making a model of part of an aircraft wing. Cut a piece of paper 200 mm long and 100 mm wide. Bend it in half as in the picture, and stick the edges together. Run a fold along the edge with your finger-nails so that it bends, curved at the top and almost flat underneath. The fold is the *leading edge*, the other the *trailing edge*, of the wing.

Make a hole straight through both parts of the wing 25 mm from the leading edge and pass a piece of drinking straw through it, fixing it with a dab of glue. A piece of light paper stuck to the trailing edge will act as a rudder. Thread smooth twine through the straw and fix it on two sticks.

As you swing the sticks through the air the wing will

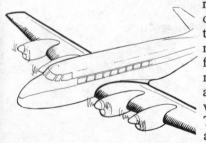

rise on the thread. The top of the wing is longer than the bottom, so the air moving over the top has further to go, and therefore moves faster. This produces a lower pressure on top of the wing, and so results in *lift*. This is how a wing helps an aeroplane to rise into the air.

38

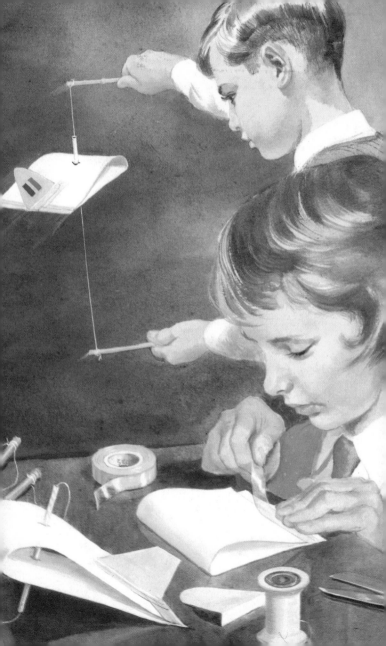

The Propeller

We have seen that a wing lifts when air passes over it, and that a bird or a glider can stay in the air when its wings are facing the wind. But an aeroplane has to fly when there is no wind, or when the wind is blowing in any direction. For the wings to lift it, it must be moved through the air, as you moved your wing-section.

A bird moves by using its wings to drive it along, an aeroplane is driven by a propeller or a jet. First we will find out about the propeller.

A propeller is really a screw which is turned by an engine. It *screws* its way into the air, pulling itself and the aircraft through the air just as a wood-screw pulls itself into wood when it is turned. In the same way, if you hold a nut and turn the bolt it pulls itself through the nut.

A ship's propeller works in the same way. As the aeroplane propeller *screws* through the air, so a ship's propeller *screws* its way through the water.

To make a propeller, get a block of soft wood about 150 mm by 25 mm by 25 mm. Make a hole in the exact middle. Cut the blades, (always cutting *away* from yourself), so that they are at opposite angles to each other. Smooth, trim and sand-paper the propeller, studying the various stages as shown in the picture.

A ship's propeller

40

Jet Flight

Two simple experiments will help you to understand how jet aeroplanes fly. Blow up a balloon, pinch the neck and suddenly let go. What happens? The balloon is driven about at great speed by the air squirting out. If you have a pair of roller skates, put them on and stand on a smooth surface. Hold a brick or a heavy lump of stone and throw it hard in front of you. You will move backwards, and the harder you throw the weight the further back you will be driven.

A jet engine throws back hot gases and thrusts the aeroplane forward. What happens is that air is drawn into the front of the engine and is used to burn paraffin fuel. This forms a gas which expands very rapidly and rushes out of the rear of the engine, producing what is called *thrust*. This drives the aeroplane forward with tremendous power, very much more than the power of a propeller.

Jet engines work best at great height, where the air is  thin and therefore easier to fly through. But there is a limit to the height at which a jet plane can fly, because it must have air to provide the oxygen to burn its fuel. The jet engine, developed during the 1939-45 war, revolutionised the design, speed and performance of the aeroplane.

Space Rockets

As we go upwards from the earth's surface the air gets thinner until, at something like 322 km up, the atmosphere ends; there is no air and we are in space. A propeller driven aeroplane cannot fly above a certain height, because the air is too thin for the propeller to *bite* into. There is a limit for jets, too, when there is not enough air to burn the fuel. Also when the air is too thin, there is not enough to flow over the wings to give the plane *lift*.

That is why, when we want to send something into space, we have to use another method. The answer is the rocket. Like the jet, the rocket throws out hot gases, but it takes its own oxygen with it. So a space rocket motor can burn its fuel and produce its tremendous thrust far away in space beyond the atmosphere.

Rockets are used to hurl space-craft through the atmosphere into space. Once out of the atmosphere there is no air to offer resistance and much less thrust is needed. Rocket motors too, are used to steer and control the craft.

The rockets we send up on Guy Fawkes night are filled with chemicals. When the touch-paper is lighted the chemicals burn, produce rapidly expanding gases, and the rocket shoots up. That is how a space-craft is launched, although, of course, it needs special fuel and great scientific accuracy and skill.

44

Air Resistance

Take two sheets of paper and screw one up as tightly as you can. Stand on a chair or table and let the sheet of paper and the screwed-up ball fall at the same time. You will find that the ball of paper will hit the ground first. *Why?*

This is because of the air resistance. Air is real and will slow down anything moving through it. There is much more air resistance to the open sheet of paper, so it falls more slowly. Air resistance gets greater as the speed of an object increases. Anything which moves fast through the air, such as an aeroplane, a motor car, or a railway engine, is designed to offer as little resistance as possible—it is *streamlined*. The special shape allows the air to flow smoothly over it. You see wonderful examples of streamlining with birds.

If, on the other hand, we want to make something slow up as it falls through the air, we increase its air resistance, as with a parachute.

Make a toy parachute with a piece of light cloth, with thread joining the corners, and hang something on it, such as a toy soldier. Fold the parachute up into a small ball and throw it up as high as you can. On the way up it offers little resistance, but when it begins to fall and opens out, it is slowed by air resistance, and floats gently downwards.

Flying a Kite

When you are flying a kite the tug on the string is caused by the resistance of the kite to the wind, to the moving air against its surface.

You can make a simple kite by following the instructions at the bottom of the page. Make a rigid frame of light thin slats of wood, or pieces of garden cane. Tie them together with strong thread where they cross. You then join the ends of the sticks with thread.

Lay a piece of grease-proof paper, newspaper, or silk on the floor, put the framework of the kite on top and cut out the shape, leaving about 25 mm all round. Fold this edge over the thread and paste it firmly.

Turn the kite over and attach two strings to the long strut, *through* the paper or silk, to make the 'bridle'. One string should be about 75 mm from the top of the long strut, the other about 300 mm from the bottom. It is to these that you fix your ball of string. Finally make the 'tail' with a piece of newspaper screwed on to a length of twine.

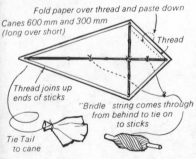

Fold paper over thread and paste down
Canes 600 mm and 300 mm
(long over short)
Thread
Thread joins up ends of sticks
"Bridle string comes through from behind to tie on to sticks
Tie Tail to cane

You need a steady wind to fly your kite, and you must experiment with the length of the 'bridle' and the tail. You launch it by running and letting the string through your fingers, and then you 'tug' it higher and higher, paying out string as needed.

Air and Sound

Without air ours would be a completely silent world, because all sounds reach our ears through the air. Sounds are produced by *vibration*. When you pluck a tight elastic band it vibrates, and sets the air vibrating. These vibrations reach your ear-drums, and set them vibrating so that you hear the sound made by the elastic band.

All sounds travel through the air, from the deep siren of a great ship to the tiny noise of an insect in the grass. Musical instruments depend on vibration, whether it is from the tightly stretched strings of a violin or from the vibration of air in the pipe of an organ. When you beat a drum you can feel the vibrations of the drum-skin.

You can make all sorts of musical instruments, such as the home-made 'banjo' in the picture. Blow across the top of an empty bottle, and make a musical note. Pour a little water in and blow again; you get a higher note. Add more water, the note is higher still.

When you blow you make the air in the bottle vibrate. When you put in some water there is less air to vibrate, so it vibrates faster and gives a higher note. The more water in the bottle, the less air, the faster it will vibrate and the higher the note will be.

50

Here is a list of the things [you]
will need for the experiment[s in]
this book. You will probably [have]
most of them.

A candle

A rubber tube

String and strong thread

A cork and a cotton reel

Several bottles and jars

A tumbler and beaker

A bowl or bucket

Pieces of wood and wooden str[ips]

A small funnel

Sticking tape and glue